RISKY JOBS

SOLDIER

JENNA TOLLI

PowerKiDS press

Published in 2025 by The Rosen Publishing Group, Inc.
2544 Clinton Street, Buffalo, NY 14224

First Edition

Editor: Jenna Tolli
Book Design: Rachel Rising

Photo Credits: Cover, Michele Ursi/Shutterstock.com; Cover, pp. 1, 3–24 Apostrophe/Shutterstock.com; Cover, pp. 1, 3, 4, 6, 8, 14, 20, 22–24 cobalt88/Shutterstock.com; Cover, pp. 1, 3–24 ReVelStockArt/Shutterstock.com; p. 5 Mie Ahmt/Shutterstock.com; pp. 7, 9 PRESSLAB/Shutterstock.com; p. 8 https://commons.wikimedia.org/wiki/File:Mark_of_the_United_States_Army.svg; p.10 https://en.m.wikipedia.org/wiki/File:Emblem_of_the_United_States_Navy.svg; p. 11 a katz/Shutterstock.com; p. 12 https://commons.wikimedia.org/wiki/File:Emblem_of_the_United_States_Marine_Corps.svg; p. 13 Yeongsik Im/Shutterstock.com; p. 14 https://en.wikipedia.org/wiki/File:Seal_of_the_U.S._Coast_Guard.svg; p. 15 RCPPHOTO/Shutterstock.com; p. 16 https://commons.wikimedia.org/wiki/File:Mark_of_the_United_States_Air_Force.svg; p. 17 Neptune's Aperture/Shutterstock.com; p. 18 https://en.wikipedia.org/wiki/File:Seal_of_the_United_States_Space_Force_(black_alternate).svg; p. 19 Rosemarie Mosteller/Shutterstock.com; p. 21 Prostock-studio/Shutterstock.com.

Library of Congress Cataloging-in-Publication Data

Names: Tolli, Jenna, author.
Title: Soldier / Jenna Tolli.
Description: Buffalo, New York : PowerKids Press, [2025] | Series: Risky jobs | Includes index.
Identifiers: LCCN 2024007330 (print) | LCCN 2024007331 (ebook) | ISBN 9781499446197 (library binding) | ISBN 9781499446180 (paperback) | ISBN 9781499446203 (ebook)
Subjects: LCSH: United States–Armed Forces–Vocational guidance–Juvenile literature.
Classification: LCC UB147 .T65 2025 (print) | LCC UB147 (ebook) | DDC 355.0023/73–dc23/eng/20240216
LC record available at https://lccn.loc.gov/2024007330
LC ebook record available at https://lccn.loc.gov/2024007331

Manufactured in the United States of America

CONTENTS

THE U.S. ARMED FORCES

U.S. military forces are meant to keep the country safe and protect its citizens. There are six U.S. military branches. These are the U.S. Army, Navy, Marine Corps, Coast Guard, Air Force, and Space Force.

Each branch uses different terms for its members. People can use the word "soldier" to mean a service member in any branch. However, it usually means a member of the U.S. Army. In the U.S. Navy, service members are sailors. Service members in the U.S. Marine Corps are marines. Service members in the U.S. Coast Guard are coastguardsmen. Service members in the U.S. Air Force are airmen. In the U.S. Space Force, service members are guardians.

DANGER!

The National Guard is another part of the military. It handles **emergencies** in communities throughout the country. The president or state governors can call in the National Guard.

Each branch of the military protects the security of the United States. Members have special training to protect the country from **threats** and war.

TRAINING AND SAFETY

Boot camp is when recruits, or new members, train to prepare for military careers. It is the first step in joining any branch of the military. In boot camp, recruits train and do very hard exercises to get into shape. They may learn how to operate military planes, helicopters, vehicles, or boats. They also learn how to use and take care of military weapons.

Troops in **combat** wear clothes called body armor. Body armor helps protect them from enemy fire. It may stop bullets from killing the person wearing it. They also wear helmets and masks for protection.

DANGER!

In the military reserves, people train for the military but work in **civilian** jobs. They go to training throughout the year. The military calls them to serve when they're needed.

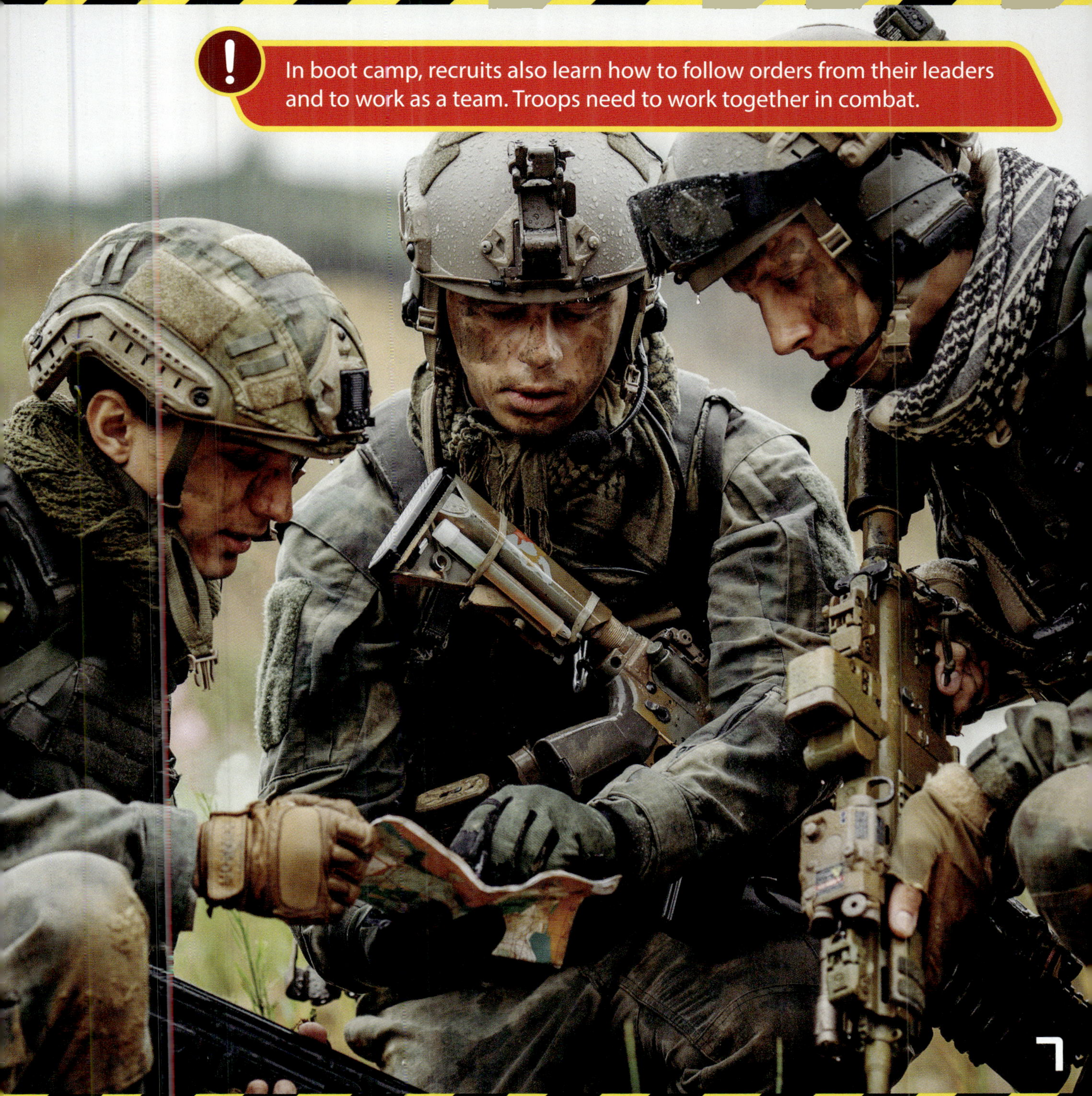

In boot camp, recruits also learn how to follow orders from their leaders and to work as a team. Troops need to work together in combat.

ARMY

The U.S. Army protects the land. It's the largest branch of the military. Like other service members, soldiers may fight in wars to defend, or protect, the country against enemies.

In infantry **units**, soldiers are trained to use guns and other small weapons. Those in the infantry fight on foot. These are troops on the ground that get close to the people they are fighting.

Artillery units use bigger weapons, like cannons or missiles. These weapons can be used from farther away to hit targets. They stay farther away from the combat zones than soldiers in infantry units.

DANGER!

Some soldiers train for the U.S. Special Forces, known as the Green Berets. Green Berets are **experts** in war and handling **terrorists**. They take part in very dangerous **missions**.

When a service member is called to serve in a war or on a mission, it's called getting deployed. When someone is deployed, they might be gone for six months, a year, or longer.

NAVY

The U.S. Navy protects the seas. Active-duty sailors work on naval bases or ships all over the world. Being on active duty means working full time in the military.

The navy uses ships, submarines, and aircraft. It also uses aircraft carriers, which are large ships used to carry airplanes and helicopters that can take off at sea. Thousands of sailors can work on a single aircraft carrier.

The Navy SEALs are the Navy's special forces unit. Navy SEALs handle important, dangerous, and sometimes secret missions. They go through special training to learn skills and handle high-risk situations.

There are over 340,000 active-duty service members in the U.S. Navy.

MARINE CORPS

The U.S. Marine Corps handles missions on the ground and at sea. The Marine Corps is a part of the Department of the Navy.

Marines **specialize** in amphibious warfare. "Amphibious" means that something is both in water and on land. They are stationed, or assigned, to places throughout the United States and all over the world.

Marines are often the first U.S. troops to arrive in areas of conflict. They go through special training to fight in the most dangerous places. There is a martial arts training program to teach marines hand-to-hand fighting skills.

Marine recruits train for about three months. They learn how to use weapons and handle emergencies they might face.

COAST GUARD

The U.S. Coast Guard protects ports, coasts, and waterways. It makes sure people follow the laws of these areas. This helps our borders stay safe.

The Coast Guard also handles search and rescue missions. This is when a person or boat is missing, or if a plane crashes and might be lost in the water. The Coast Guard looks for people and helps bring them to safety.

When the country isn't at war, the Coast Guard operates as part of the Department of Homeland Security. During times of war, it operates under the Department of the Navy.

DANGER!

Every day, the Coast Guard opens over 40 search and rescue cases on average. It also checks hundreds of boats coming into the United States to be sure they're safe.

The Coast Guard uses boats, airplanes, and helicopters for its work.

AIR FORCE

The U.S. Air Force uses different kinds of aircraft to complete missions. Fighter planes are very fast and can be used to fight other aircraft. The air force also uses planes and helicopters to take service members wherever they are needed. Some service members in the air force fly and others work on the ground.

Not all pilots fly in combat. Test pilots fly new airplanes and try out different ways of flying them. They can tell the air force whether a new plane or a flight move is safe. They test the limits of the planes they fly, which can be very dangerous.

Air Force pararescue teams find and rescue military members. They can get them out of danger and help treat them if they're hurt.

SPACE FORCE

The U.S. Space Force was created in 2019 to help with security in space. It is the first new U.S. military branch to be created in over 70 years.

Today, we have more ways to learn about space and space travel than we ever have before. People around the world also use **satellites** in space to communicate. Unfortunately, there could be people who want to harm these **resources** in space. They could even stop other people from going into space. The Space Force was created to defend the United States against these threats and protect our work in space.

The U.S. Space Force motto, or saying, is "Semper Supra" which is Latin for "always above."

DEFENDING THE NATION

Service members risk their lives to protect the United States and its people. When soldiers or other service members join the military, they might be called on to fight in a war. They know they could get hurt or killed in combat or on a mission. There are different risks and dangers in each branch of the military. There are also many types of jobs within each branch.

Above all, members of the U.S. military are proud to know that they defend our country against enemies. This can take a lot of courage. They put themselves in danger to keep everyone safe.

DANGER!

Many active-duty military members have lost their lives during their service. They are respected and honored for dedicating their lives to protecting our country.

Service members wear dress uniforms on special occasions. Each military branch has different combat uniforms and dress uniforms.

GLOSSARY

artillery: The part of an army that uses large guns, such as cannons, or other guns.

civilian: A person not on active duty in the military.

combat: A battle or a fight.

emergency: An unexpected situation that calls for immediate action.

expert: Someone who has a special skill or knowledge.

mission: A special job or task.

resource: Something that can be used.

satellite: A spacecraft placed in orbit around Earth, a moon, or a planet to collect information or to be used for communication.

specialize: To focus on something.

terrorist: A person who uses violence to scare people as a way of achieving a political goal.

threat: A person or thing that may cause others to be hurt or killed.

unit: A group of soldiers.

FOR MORE INFORMATION

BOOKS

Billings, Tanner. *The U.S. Army.* New York, NY: Rosen Publishing, 2022.

Miller, Janice. *Combat Experts.* Vero Beach, FL: Rourke Educational Media, 2021.

Phillips, Howard. *Inside the Navy SEALs.* New York, NY: PowerKids Press, 2022.

WEBSITES

U.S. Department of Defense
www.defense.gov/about/our-forces
Explore each military branch's website to learn more.

United States Space Force
www.spaceforce.com
Learn about the newest branch of the military, the U.S. Space Force.

Publisher's note to educators and parents: Our editors have carefully reviewed these websites to ensure that they are suitable for students. Many websites change frequently, however, and we cannot guarantee that a site's future contents will continue to meet our high standards of quality and educational value. Be advised that students should be closely supervised whenever they access the internet.

INDEX